BASKETBALL is the most popular spectator sport in the United States, and the second most popular sport in the world. For participants and spectators this addition to the **Young People's Sports Dictionary** Series is a must.

The rules and terminology of basketball are concisely defined and the history of the sport is interestingly described. The humorous sketches bring enjoyment to youngsters while adding clarity to the text.

Manuel Moreno Guzmán

ILLUSTRATED BASKETBALL
DICTIONARY FOR YOUNG PEOPLE

ILLUSTRATED BASKETBALL DICTIONARY FOR YOUNG PEOPLE

BY STEVE CLARK

ILLUSTRATED BY
FRANK BAGINSKI

PRENTICE-HALL, INC.
Englewood Cliffs, New Jersey

Illustrated Basketball Dictionary for Young People
by Steve Clark
Copyright © 1977 by Harvey House
Treehouse Paperback edition published 1978 by Prentice-Hall,
Inc. by arrangement with Harvey House, Publishers

Library of Congress Catalog Card Number 77-77859
Printed in the United States of America • J
ISBN 0-13-450940-4
10 9 8 7 6 5 4 3 2 1

Foreword

TODAY, the exciting game of basketball ranks second only to soccer as the most popular sport in the world.

Here in the United States, more people play basketball than any other team game, and basketball—not football—is our most popular spectator sport. Each winter, millions of fans jam into huge coliseums, gymnasiums and sleek arenas to watch high school, college and professional basketball games. It's difficult for today's sports fans to believe that this lively game began with just a couple of dusty peach baskets and a beat-up soccer ball.

Back in the 1890's, young people did not have a popular sport to play during the long winter months. They played baseball in the spring and summer and football in the fall, but when cold winter winds blew and snow covered the playing fields, there was nothing they could do except stay indoors. Many did physical exercises to keep fit, but that wasn't much fun.

In November of 1891, a young physical education teacher named Dr. James A. Naismith was assigned to a troublesome class. He was teaching at the YMCA Training School (now Springfield College) in Springfield, Massachusetts, and his students were bored with indoor calisthenics, leap frog, tumbling and other gym games. They were restless and wanted something more exciting to play.

Dr. Naismith began thinking about inventing a new game for the students, one that they could play indoors. He decided on a game that would involve throwing a ball at a target. Footballs and rugby balls were pointed and hard to handle, so he chose a soft leather soccer ball for his game. Then he went down into the school's basement and rummaged around for a target. He found two dusty, wooden peach baskets. They would catch the soccer ball perfectly if it was tossed in the right way. With help from the school janitors, Dr. Naismith nailed the baskets to the gym balcony, one at each end.

That night, he went home and made up 13 basic rules for his game. He explained the rules to his class the next day in the gym. The students began passing the soccer ball quickly from one to the other. Around and around the ball went until one of the students stopped and tossed the ball into the peach basket. That's how basketball was born.

Dr. Naismith's game has come a long way since the peach basket days. Basketball's language has come a long way, too. This dictionary contains the basketball terms and phrases used by today's players, coaches, announcers and sportswriters. Outdated words have been omitted.

A

Advancing the ball—Before a shot at the basket can be tried, a team must move the ball from one end of the playing court to the other. The ball may be legally advanced by passing or dribbling.

Air ball—An attempted shot at the basket that sails through the air and fails to touch the rim, net, or backboard.

All-American team—An All-Star team selected each year by sportswriters and coaches from all parts of the country. The team consists of the best college players of that particular year.

All-Conference team—Every year, college coaches and professional sportswriters throughout the country select the best players in each conference (geographic zone). These players receive special awards at the end of the playing season. This is only an *honorary* team; it plays no actual games.

All-Professional team—Each year professional coaches and sportswriters pick the best players from the ranks of the professional NBA.

Arc—The most important fundamental to remember when learning how to toss a basketball at a basket. The ball should curve up before it comes down into the basket.

B

Backboard—The backstop which holds the rim and net. Some backboards are fan-shaped, but most are rectangular. The backboard is usually attached to a tall pole or support at a height of 10 feet above the ground. Some are suspended from gymnasium ceilings. Early backboards were wooden. While some of today's backboards are still made of wood, many are made of clear plastic.

Back court—The half of the court farthest from the basket that a team is attacking, including the division line. A division line divides front court from back court.

Back-door play—An offensive move in which a closely guarded player runs away from the basket to receive a pass, then suddenly reverses direction and heads for the basket to receive the pass.

This play is used to fool an overanxious defensive player. (See illustration)

Balanced offense—A system of scoring plays that puts some offensive team members in good shooting positions and others in good rebounding positions in case shots are missed.

Ball—A basketball is perfectly round and may be made of rubber or leather. Its circumference is 29½ to 30 inches. Basketballs of long ago were made of stitched leather. Today's basketballs are molded and have smooth surfaces.

Ball control—An offensive passing system used to keep possession of the ball until good scoring plays can be set up.

Ball handling—Passing, catching, dribbling, and controlling the ball without losing possession.

Ball hawk—An aggressive defensive player, especially one who often steals the ball from opponents.

Bank shot—A shot, usually taken from an angle, which bounces against the backboard just above the rim and falls into the basket.

Baseball pass—A one-handed pass thrown with the same overhand motion used to throw a baseball. It is often used as the first pass of a fast break.

Baseline—The line and the floor area from sideline to sideline under each basket.

Basket—The basket ring, or rim, is 18 inches in diameter and is attached to a backboard.

Basket hanger—A player who is always near his offensive basket or who runs to his basket for unguarded shots.

Behind-the-back pass—A difficult pass thrown by advanced players. The ball is brought around the player's back with one hand and, in the same motion, passed to a teammate.

Biddy Basketball—Special basketball leagues for boys ages 9 to 12 and girls ages 9 to 13. These players must be no more than 5 feet 6 inches tall.

Blind pass—A pass to a teammate made by a player who is looking in another direction. This is a dangerous pass and is often intercepted.

Blocked shot—An attempted shot at the basket that is knocked away by a defensive player after the ball has left the hand of the shooter and before the ball has started to come down into the basket.

Blocking—An illegal play which impedes the progress of an opponent.

Blocking out—Used by defensive players to keep the offensive players away from the basket after a missed shot. The defensive players turn their backs into the offensive players and block them away from the basket area.

Blowing a shot—Missing an easy try for a basket.

Bomb—A long shot at the basket, usually a set shot taken by a guard.

Bounce pass—A pass which is bounced on the floor from one offensive player to another. This pass is most often used against a zone defense or to begin a layup shot.

Box-and-one defense—Four defensive players play a box-shaped zone and try to get the ball by intercepting passes. The remaining defensive player plays man-to-man defense, guarding the other team's best shooter. (See illustration)

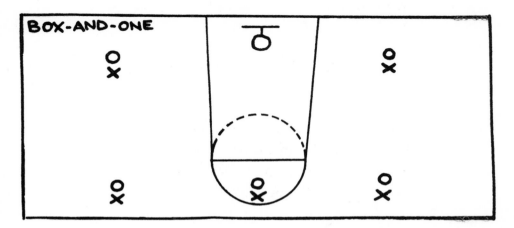

Boxer's shuffle—A sliding step used by defensive players for moving quickly in any direction. The feet are shuffled quickly and are always kept in contact with the floor. (See illustration)

2 3

Boxing out—Another term for *Blocking out*. Some coaches prefer to use the term *Boxing out* when instructing their players.

Breakaway—When a player sneaks down-court ahead of the other team and receives a pass from a teammate. This play is used as part of a fast break.

Buffer Zone—Another term for free throw lane.

Burning the nets—A phrase used when a player makes basket after basket without missing.

C

Center—This offensive player, also called the pivot player, plays near the basket. The center is usually the tallest player on a team.

Center jump—An official tosses the ball up between the best jumpers of each team, usually the centers, and each jumper tries to tap the ball to his teammates. The players must tap the ball, not grab it. The other members of both teams must stay outside the center circle during the jump. The center jump is used to begin play at the start of each new quarter and half. In the NBA, a center jump is used only to start each game.

Change-up—A change of pace or speed while dribbling or running.

Charity stripe—Another name for the free throw line.

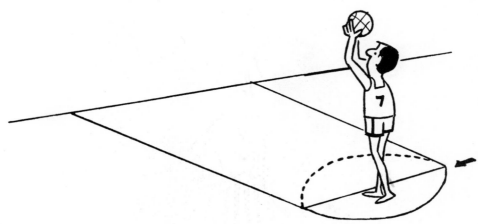

Chart—A special sheet of paper or notebook used by coaches to record the shots, rebounds, errors, and other statistics of the players.

Chaser—The front player in a zone defense whose duty is to harass the attacking team's players and force them to make bad passes.

Check-off—A defensive maneuver in which two players of the defensive team quickly swap the offensive players they are supposed to guard.

Chest pass—A two-handed pass thrown from chest level.

Chest shot—A one- or two-handed shot begun at chest level. This shot is usually tossed at the basket from far out in the court.

Clear out—Four offensive players moving to one side of the playing court to allow their remaining teammate to make a play by himself. When the four offensive players move to one side, they draw the defensive players with them. This gives the remaining offensive player a larger area in which to make a play.

Clogging the middle—A defensive team maneuver in which the players gather in front of the offensive team's basket forcing the offensive players to take long shots rather than easy layup shots.

CLOGGING THE MIDDLE

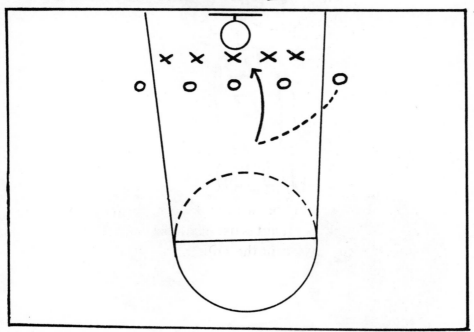

Closely guarded—Term used to describe defensive players playing unusually close to the offensive players.

Coach—The organizer, teacher, and leader of a team. Usually a nonplaying member, the coach sits on the players' bench during a game and plans and directs the team's strategy.

Conditioning—Exercises and drills used by a coach to put his team in top physical condition.

Conference—Another term for league.

Continuation play—A player who is fouled by a defensive player at the beginning of a layup shot receives credit for the basket if the ball goes in.

Cornerman—An offensive player whose position is normally to the side of the basket near the corner of the playing court.

Corner shot—A difficult attempt at the basket taken from a corner of the court. Because the shot is taken from the side, the shooter has only the rim, not the backboard, to aim at.

Court—Another term for the basketball playing area. The size of the court depends upon the age group of the players. High school players use a court 84 feet long and 50 feet wide. College and professional teams play on a court 94 feet long and 50 feet wide. Each of these courts has two backboards and baskets, one at each end of the playing area. In the center of the court is a jump circle where center jumps begin each new quarter and half. There is a free throw line and free throw circle at each end of the court. Two lines connect each free throw line to the baselines. The area inside these lines is called the buffer zone, or free throw lane. (See court diagrams)

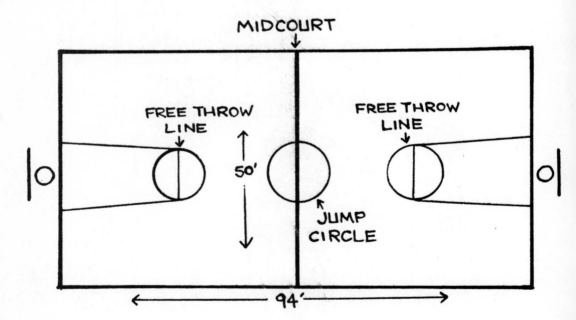

Covering a man—Playing defense against an opposing player.

Crack the defense—Finding a weakness in the defense of the other team. The offensive team then uses scoring plays to take advantage of this defensive weakness. For example, if an offensive team's forward is too quick for the defensive forward who is guarding him, the offensive team uses plays that take advantage of their forward's quickness.

Crash the boards—Grabbing the ball after a teammate has missed a shot and trying to get a second and third attempt at the basket. This play usually results in plenty of body contact as players from both teams try to get the ball.

Crisscross play—Two members of the offensive team run past a teammate who has the ball, each player running in a different direction. They form a crisscross pattern in front of the player with the ball.

This play is used to confuse the defensive players. Once the defensive players are confused, at least one of the offensive team players is usually free to receive a pass from the player with the ball.

Crossover dribble—This play is used by a player with the ball in order to change the direction in which he is dribbling and to confuse the defensive players nearest him. The player dribbling the ball suddenly bounces it in front of him, changes dribbling hands, and continues to dribble with his other hand. (See illustration)

Cutting—Moving quickly towards the basket hoping to receive a pass from a teammate.

D

Dead ball—When the ball is not in play, such as during a timeout.

Deadly shooter—A very good shooter who seldom misses.

Defense—Trying to stop the other team from scoring or advancing the ball.

Defensive signals—Instructions given to the defensive team members by their captain or coach. Some teams change defensive strategy during a game by using signals. This often confuses the offensive team.

Defensive stance—The correct positions of the hands and feet a player should have while guarding another player. The player should crouch slightly and spread his feet so he is comfortable and able to move quickly to each side. The hands should be held low with the palms open and facing upwards. (See illustration)

Defensive system—The defense strategy a coach wants his players to use against a specific team.

After he finds out the other team's playing strengths (such as great shooting or rebounding), the coach picks the defense he believes will effectively resist those strengths and stop the other team from scoring. The coach might change his defensive plan during a game if the other team changes any of its offensive players.

Defensive triangle—Positioning three defensive players in a triangle under the basket to block out the other team. The players then try to get rebounds from missed shots. (See illustration)

Delay of game—Preventing the ball from being promptly made alive, or allowing the game to develop into an actionless contest. Also, taking too much time in a timeout huddle after the official has signalled for the game to continue.

Diamond-and-one—A type of defense similar to the *Box-and-one*. Four defensive players play a diamond-shaped zone defense. The remaining defensive player plays man-to-man defense, guarding the other team's best shooter. (See illustration)

DIAMOND-AND-ONE

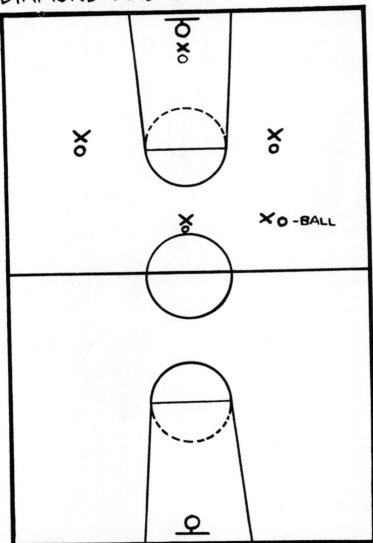

Disqualified player—A player who has reached the limit of fouls allowed by the rules. This player must leave the game and cannot return. In amateur basketball, a player is disqualified when he has fouled five times. Six is the limit in the NBA professional league.

Donkey basketball—A funny variation of basketball in which the players ride on donkeys. The donkeys do the running and the players do the shooting.

Double dribble—Dribbling again after having already stopped. Also, dribbling with two hands at the same time. Both types of double dribbling are illegal.

Double foul—This occurs when two players, one from each team, make a foul at the same time. Nobody receives free throws. Instead, there is a center jump.

Double-header game—When two different games are scheduled at different times on the same day in the same arena.

Double pivot—An offensive system of play using two centers or pivot players. This system is usually used by teams having two or more very tall players.

Double screen—Two offensive players standing close together in front of a teammate who is taking a clear shot at the basket. The two players keep the defense away from the shooter.

Double-team—Two defensive players guarding one offensive player.

Downcourt—The far end of the court away from the action.

Down the middle—An offensive play in which an offensive player runs or dribbles down the foul lane towards the basket.

Dribbling—Moving the ball across the floor by bouncing it. When a player taps the ball with *one* hand so that it bounces on the floor, this is called a *dribble*. A player can dribble once or any number of times before stopping. Once stopped, the player cannot continue dribbling; he must pass or shoot the ball. (See illustration)

Drive-in—When an offensive player with the ball dribbles to the basket for a layup shot.

Driving layup—The twisting, spinning layup shot at the end of a drive-in play.

Dummy play—A player who is about to receive a pass from a teammate does not try to catch the ball until the last moment. This play is used to fool an unsuspecting defensive player who does not realize that a pass has been thrown.

Dunking the ball—An offensive play in which a player with the ball jumps and jams the ball down into the basket. Dunking can be dangerous and can result in an injury to the player involved.

E

End lines—The lines under each basket that connect the sidelines. The end line is also called the baseline.

Excessive timeout—When a team calls more timeouts than are allowed by the rules, the other team receives a free throw. In amateur basketball, teams are allowed five timeouts per game.

Extra period—An extra playing period used when the regular game ends with a tie score. Professional and college extra periods are five minutes long. High school teams play three minute extra periods.

Eye fakes—Movements with the eyes used by offensive players to fake a defensive player out of position.

F

Fakes and feints—Tricky moves of the eyes, head, and/or body; they are used to throw an opponent off balance.

Fall away shot—An off-balance shot taken while falling away from the basket. This move is used to prevent a shot from being blocked.

Fancy Dan—Description given to a player who makes fancy plays and shots just to please the crowd.

Fast break—A type of offense used to move the ball quickly toward the basket before the defensive team can get there to prevent a play. It begins as soon as a team gets the ball. The ball is passed or dribbled in the middle of the court by an offensive player who is running towards his team's basket. At the same time two or more teammates run at top speed toward the basket, one near each sideline. When the basket is reached, the player with the ball can pass to either teammate or shoot the ball himself.

Field goal—A successful attempt at the basket, but not a free throw. A field goal counts two points.

Firehouse basketball—Description given to the fastest of the fast break systems. In this type of fast break, all five players run at top speed toward the basket.

Five-man fast break—A type of fast break in which each of the players has a special job to do. It is an organized rush to the basket, not a wild scramble like *Firehouse basketball*.

Five-man weave—All five offensive players controlling the ball by passing and moving in a sliding pattern near the center of the court. This controlled system is sometimes used as a stall or delay tactic when a team is leading. (See illustration)

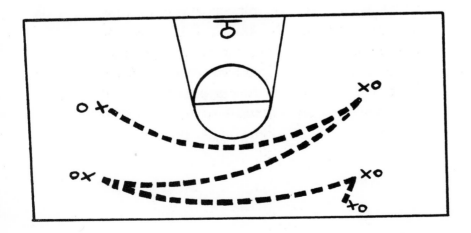

Floating—Guarding an offensive player in such a way that you can cover him yet still be in a position to help teammates with their guarding, if necessary.

Floating a pass—Making a high, soft pass that is easy to intercept.

Follow-through—Following the flight of the ball with the arms after passing or shooting.

Footwork—Learning how to slide the feet across the floor instead of just running. When sliding, the feet should keep contact with the floor. This is an important fundamental.

Formation—The lineup of players in offensive or defensive positions.

Forward—Another term for cornerman.

Forward wall—Description of the tall players of a team (the center and the two forwards) who play near the basket.

Foul—An infraction or breaking of the rules for which a penalty is charged.

Foul shot—Another term for free throw.

Free throw—A free shot given to a player because of a foul by the opposing team.

Free throw lane—The area inside the large rectangle under each basket. On offense, a player cannot remain inside this area for more than three seconds. Players often run across this area looking for passes from their teammates. The lane used by the NBA professional league is 16 feet wide. In amateur basketball the lane is 12 feet wide.

FREE THROW LANE

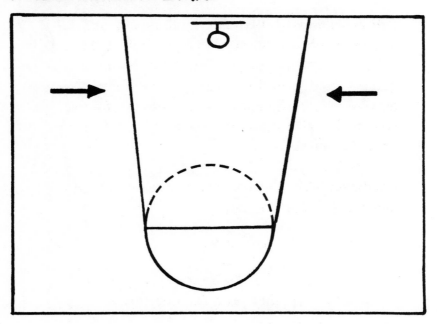

Free throw line—A line in front of each basket where players stand to shoot free throws. The line is 15 feet from the backboard.

Freeze—An attempt by the offensive team to keep possession of the ball until time runs out. Amateur rules allow a team to freeze the ball for a long time. In the NBA, however, the offensive team must attempt a shot within 24 seconds or lose possession of the ball.

Full court—The entire court area from end line to end line.

Full court press—An exciting defensive system in which the defensive players guard the offensive players very closely. The defensive players use the entire court to harass the offensive players. The defense hopes the offensive team will make mistakes such as bad passes or violations.

Fundamentals—The basic rules, strategy, and techniques of basketball.

G

Getting position—A quick move by a player to a spot on the court from which he can make a good play.

Girls' basketball—Today, basketball is a recognized and popular team sport for girls as well as boys. Many high schools and colleges have girls' and boys' basketball teams, and the rules they follow are almost identical. In girls' college basketball, however, a 30-second shooting clock is used.

Give-and-go—An offensive play in which one player gives the ball to a teammate and then runs to the basket looking for a return pass.

Goal tending—An attempt by the defense to block a shot after the ball has started to come down into the basket. The official then signals that goal tending has been committed and that the basket counts.

Green player—Description given to an inexperienced player. Such a player is also called a rookie.

Guard—A member of the offensive team who plays away from the basket and directs the offensive system. Guards are usually quick on their feet and good ball handlers.

Guarding—Another term for covering a man. (See illustration)

Gunner—A selfish offensive player who shoots too much and doesn't pass the ball to his teammates.

H

Half—A game is divided into halves. High school games have four 8-minute quarters (each half is 16 minutes long). College halves are 20 minutes in length. Professional games are divided into four 12-minute quarters (each half is 24 minutes long).

Halfcourt—One of the two halves of the court on either side of the division line.

Half time—The rest period between the two halves. High school teams rest for 10 minutes. College and professional teams have 15-minute rest periods at half time.

Handoff—One offensive player giving the ball to another.

Hand signals—A team coach or captain uses finger and hand signs to tell the team what play to use next.

Hash marks—Two little lines extending from the sidelines in each halfcourt area. A closely guarded offensive player must move past these lines within five seconds or the official will call for a jump ball. These lines are not used in the professional NBA.

Head fakes—Quick little head movements used to throw an opponent off balance.

Heady player—Description given to a smart player who takes advantage of the opposing team's mistakes.

Held ball—When a player from each team grabs the ball at the same time with one or both hands. A held ball also occurs when a closely guarded player doesn't move past the hash marks within five seconds. (See *Hash marks*) The official blows his whistle and signals for a jump ball.

Holding—Personal contact with an opponent which interferes with his freedom of movement.

Hook pass—A pass thrown with a hooking or curving motion, usually used to start a fast break.

Hook shot—A shot in which a player begins with his back to the basket, turns, and, with the shooting arm raised, flips the ball at the basket. It is the most difficult shot to stop. (See illustration)

Hoop—Another term for basket.

Hot shooter—A player who can't seem to miss when shooting at the basket.

Huddle—A group of players talking about strategy or listening to their coach.

Hustling—Playing with extra effort on both offense and defense.

I

Illegal dribble—Bouncing the ball so high that it is necessary to turn the dribbling hand over and carry the ball.

Individual plays—Offensive plays designed to give good shots to each member of the offensive team. Most individual plays are signalled for so that all members of the offensive team know which play is being used.

Inside play—Offensive plays and strategy that take place in the area under the basket.

Intentional foul—When a player purposely hits or makes an obvious foul against an opponent. This is often done to stop the clock or to bother a player who is attempting an easy layup shot. The penalty is the awarding of two free shots.

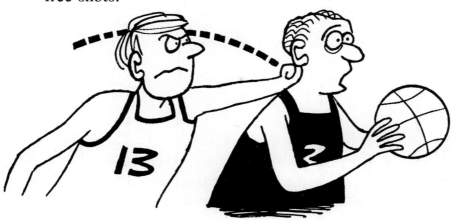

International rules—Rules of play followed when teams of different nations play against one another. These rules differ slightly from American amateur basketball rules. The major differences are: 1) a 30-second shooting clock is used; 2) the free throw lane is cone-shaped with the widest part of the cone located near the basket.

J

Jump ball—A center jump is called at the beginning of each new quarter and half, except in the professional NBA where a jump ball is used to open the game. A jump ball is also known as a held ball when one player from each team simultaneously grabs the ball with one or both hands and play stops. The official then takes the ball to the nearest jump circle and tosses it up between the two players involved.

Jump ball circle—Special circles used for jump balls. They are located at center court and at each free throw line.

Jump hook shot—A hook shot that is even more difficult to stop than a regular hook shot because the shooting player jumps straight up when tossing the ball at the basket.

Jumping jack—Description given to a player with exceptional jumping ability. This player is usually a crowd pleaser because of his ability to soar above the other players.

Jump pass—A player, while at the highest point of his jump, throws a pass from over his head.

Jump shot—The most popular shot used to-day. A player stops, jumps, and, at the highest point of his jump, tosses the ball at the hoop. (See illustration)

Junior varsity—A school team composed of young players trying to improve enough so they can play for the varsity team.

K

Key—The free throw lane and the jump ball circle attached to it. The shape of this area resembles a keyhole.

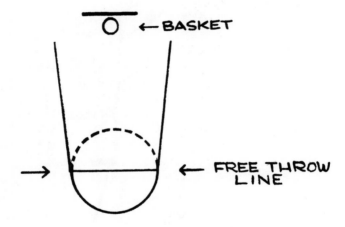

← BASKET

← FREE THROW LINE

Killing the clock—During the last few minutes of a game or period, the players of a winning or tied team may switch to an offensive system designed to use as much time as possible. In the last seconds of a game, this strategy is called a freeze.

L

Lateral pass—The ball is passed sideways across the court from one player to another.

Layup—A shot at the basket from directly under or from one side of the basket. This shot can be attempted after dribbling to the basket or after receiving a pass.

Leading the fast break—The offensive player running ahead of all other players during a fast break.

Lead pass—A chest or bounce pass deliberately thrown in front of a running player. This allows the ball to reach the speeding player rather than fall behind him.

League—A group of teams that play only each other during the season.

Lineup for a free throw—The positions taken along the free throw lane while another player is attempting a free throw.

Long shot—A try for a basket attempted from far out in the court. These shots are sometimes called "long bombs."

Looping pass—A high, soft pass that is similar to a floating pass.

Loose ball—When neither team has possession of a bouncing or rolling ball.

Loose ball foul—Occurs when a player fouls a member of the opposing team while going after a loose ball. Used only in professional basketball.

M

Man-to-man—A defensive system in which each player guards a definite player on the opposing team. The defensive players try to keep their opponents from shooting and passing.

Marking a man—Used only in international basketball, it is another way of saying *guarding a man*.

Match-ups—A strategy used by a coach to match the defensive skills of each of his players against the offensive skills of each member of the other team. This enables a team to play better man-to-man defense.

Midcourt—That part of the front court between the division line and a parallel imaginary line 28 feet from the end line.

Midcourt line—A line dividing the playing court in halves. Once the offensive team crosses this line with the ball, it cannot take the ball back across the line.

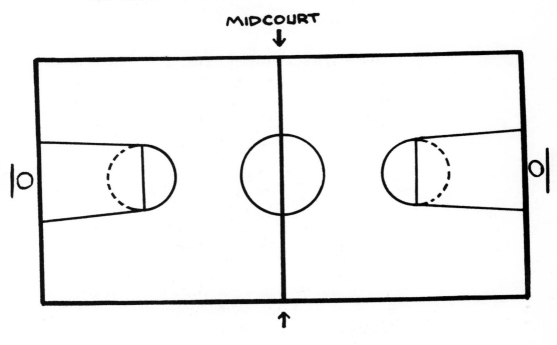

Middleman—The player who has the ball and dribbles it down the middle of the court during a fast break. (See illustration—Fast break)

N

NBA—These initials stand for the National Basketball Association, a professional league with teams in many large American cities. This league was founded in 1950.

Net—Made of white cord and hung from the rim of each basket, the net slows down the ball as it passes through the hoop.

O

Offense—The team trying to score or put the ball through the basket.

Offensive foul—When a player on the offensive team charges into or blocks a member of the defensive team.

Offensive goal tending—When an offensive player interferes with the ball as it is about to enter the basket after a shot, or touches the ball when it is balanced on the rim. Also called offensive interference.

Offensive play—Strategy designed to give the offensive team a good chance to score a basket.

Offensive system—A series of offensive plays used to attack the defensive team. The system takes advantage of the other team's defensive weaknesses.

Officials—The referee and umpire who are on the court. Both use whistles to call attention to their signals. The timer and scorekeeper assist them and occupy positions at the scorer's table.

Officials' signals—When a rule is broken by a player, either the referee or the umpire blows his whistle and uses hand and/or arm signals to describe the foul and the penalty. (See illustration)

Off-the-ball foul—A foul committed by a player or players not near the ball. Pushing and holding are common fouls of this type.

Off the court—Outside of the playing area.

One-hand shot—A try for a basket using one hand to shoot the ball.

One-three-one—A zone defense in which one player is up front near the free throw circle, three players play across the free throw line, and one player remains under the basket. (See illustration)

1-3-1

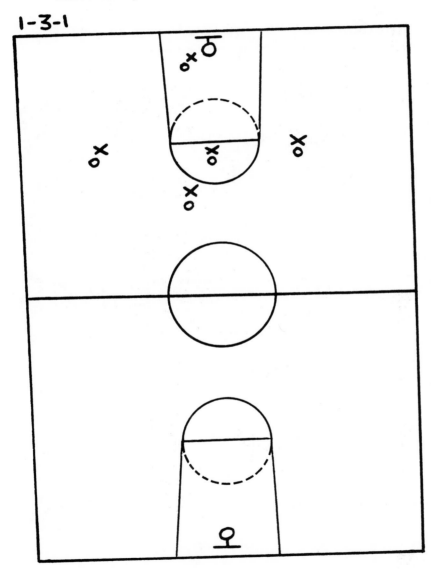

One-two-two—A zone defense in which one player is up front to harass the offensive team's ball handler, two players play near the free throw line, and two players remain under the basket. (See illustration)

1-2-2

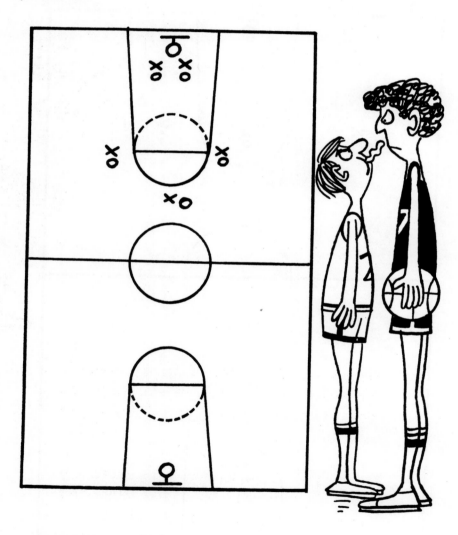

Open shot—When a player with the ball is in good position to shoot and is not being bothered by defensive players.

Option—An alternative offensive play that is used when the original play is stopped by the defensive team. Most offensive plays have several options.

Outlet pass—The first pass of a fast break. It is thrown hard and quickly by the rebounding player to a teammate near the sideline.

Out of bounds—Outside of the end lines and sidelines. When a player's foot touches or goes past one of these lines, he is out of bounds.

When the ball leaves the playing court during play and crosses the end lines or sidelines, the ball is out of bounds. The team whose player last touched the ball before it went out of bounds loses it to the other team. The officials retrieve the ball and give it to the other team at the spot on the court where the ball went out of bounds.

Outside—This is what "out of bounds" is called in international basketball.

Outside play—An offensive scoring play that begins away from the basket.

Overhead pass—A pass thrown from above the head with the arms extended. A good pass to use when passing to the center.

Overhead shot—A set shot a player takes by extending his arms over his head and throwing the ball.

Overplay—When a defensive player stays to one side of an offensive player instead of directly between the player and the basket.

Overtime—An extra period of play needed to decide the winner of a tie game.

P

Pattern play—An offensive system in which the players move in pre-planned directions on the court during an offensive play. Players using this system seldom vary the pattern in which they move.

Pep talk—An encouraging talk given to the team by the coach before the game, during a timeout, or between halves.

Personal foul—Another term for foul. Each player is allowed only a certain number of personal fouls before he becomes disqualified. Disqualified players must leave the game.

Pick—A legal block of a defensive player by an offensive player. When the player making the pick does not have the ball, he cannot move into the path of the moving defensive player too quickly. If he has the ball, he can pivot and make a legal block while handing the ball to a teammate. (See illustration)

Pick and roll—An offensive play performed by two members of the offensive team. One player makes a pick and then hands the ball to a teammate. After handing off, the player who made the pick heads for the basket hoping to receive a pass. Going to the basket after making a pick is called rolling to the basket.

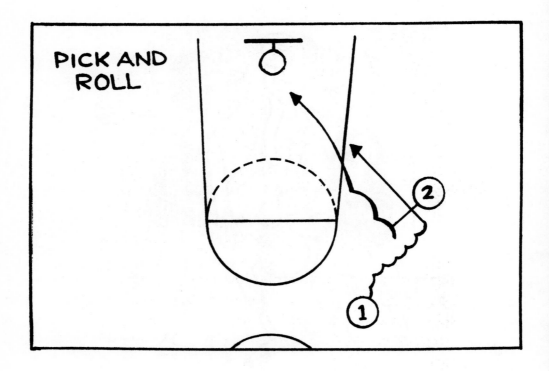

Pivoting—Making a turn of one foot. This foot, the pivot foot, must always be in contact with the floor. A pivot can be made with or without the ball.

Pivot player—Another term for a center. This player is usually tall and he usually plays near the basket.

Players' bench—Where the coach and the substitutes of a team sit while the game is in progress. The bench is usually located alongside the official scorer's table.

Playing court, amateur—Amateur playing area. These courts vary in size. High school courts measure 84 feet long and 50 feet wide. College courts are 94 feet long and 50 feet wide.

Playing court, international—Used for international games and for the Olympic Games. The free throw lane is cone-shaped, the widest part of the lane being under the basket.

Playing court, professional—Playing area for professionals. These courts are the same size as college courts. The free throw lane on a professional court is wider than amateur courts—16 feet wide.

Possession—Having the ball in order to dribble it, pass it, or attempt a shot at the basket.

Post player—A tall player, usually the center, who takes an offensive position on one side of the free throw lane or at the free throw line. Playing near the basket, this player is known as a "low post." While on the free throw line, the player is called a "high post." Many offensive scoring plays involve a post player.

Pressing—When a player, offensive or defensive, tries too hard and makes foolish mistakes.

Pressing defense—A system in which the defensive players guard the other team's offensive players very closely to cause them to make bad passes or shots. This system can be played full or half court.

Pulled hamstring—A painful leg injury common among basketball players. Hamstring muscles are located in back of each thigh.

Pushing foul—A foul usually committed by a defensive player while trying to stop a speedy offensive player. Sometimes, however, an offensive player is charged with "pushing off" while on his way to the hoop.

Pushing off—This happens when a player from one team shoves a player from another team. It usually occurs when both players are trying to get the ball. It is a foul. As a penalty, the ball is given to the team who's player was pushed.

Q

Quarter—One of four periods of actual playing time. The professionals play 12-minute quarters. High school teams play 8-minute quarters. College teams play two 20-minute halves.

R

Rebounding—Going after and getting the ball after any player has missed a basket. Both the offensive team and the defensive team try to get the missed shot. Much body contact results under the basket as players from both teams crowd each other to retrieve the ball.

Referee—One of two officials on the court who makes sure the game is played according to the rules.

Roll—Cutting quickly to the basket after making a pick. This offensive move is the second part of a play known as "pick and roll."

Rookie—A young or inexperienced player playing with a team or in a league for the first time.

Running a play—Executing or performing an offensive play.

Running right-hander—A shot at the basket made while running at top speed. The shooter jumps and tosses the ball at the hoop with his right hand.

S

Safety player—The offensive player who stays near the midcourt line while his teammates are running a play. This player guards against a quick fast break by the other team.

Sagging—Similar to floating. A defensive play made by players on the weak side of the court. These players edge to the middle of the free throw lane to be ready to help their teammates.

Scoop pass—A quick underhand pass to a teammate, often used when an offensive player is being closely guarded.

Scoreboard—Usually located overhead or on the side of the playing court. The scoreboard posts the scores of each team, the time remaining in the quarter, and, in big gymnasiums, the number of fouls committed by each player.

Scorekeepers—The official scorer and his assistants; they sit behind a table located out of bounds at midcourt. Before entering a game, players must report to the scorer.

Scoring—Giving a team credit for all successful baskets and free throws its players make during a game. Each successful basket, also called a field goal, counts for two points.

Scout—A coach, assistant coach, or member of a team who watches games played by other teams and reports the results to the head coach. Professional teams use scouts to look for college players who demonstrate potential for professional basketball.

Screen—The protection of a shooting player by a teammate or teammates. A screen temporarily keeps the defense away from the shooter. (See illustration) The player or players making a screen cannot hold or grab the defensive players.

Screen play—An offensive play designed to keep the defense away from a shooter who is taking aim at the basket from behind a screen.

Set play—A prearranged offensive play. Each player has an assigned place on the court and a specific job to do in the play. Many teams have special set plays for use during the last seconds of a game.

Set shot—When a player stops, takes aim, and "gets set" before shooting the ball. Set shots can be made with one or both hands. The two-hand shot was most popular during the early days of basketball. (See illustration)

Shooting clock—A special clock used in professional and international basketball that sets a time limit for the offensive team.

Shot chart—A written record of all shots taken during a game. The chart shows which shots were successful and the specific court location each player was in when he attempted the shot.

Shovel pass—Similar to a scoop pass. This type of pass can be made with one or both hands.

Sidelines—The long lines on the side of the playing court that connect the end lines. Any play on or outside of these lines is out of bounds.

Signals—The playing language of basketball. Coaches and captains use hand, finger and number signals to let their teams know what play or defensive system to use.

Skull session—A team meeting before a game to discuss offensive and defensive strategy. The strengths and weaknesses of the opponents are also discussed in these meetings.

Sliding—The correct movement of the feet while playing man-to-man defense. Instead of crossing one foot over the other while guarding a man, defensive players slide their feet along the floor.

Slow break—The opposite of a fast break. The offensive players take their time going down-court to play offense. This type of system is used by teams that like to use a pattern play offense.

Spinning layup—Similar to a driving layup. The offensive player dribbles down the free throw lane. While twisting his body, the player spins the ball off the backboard into the basket.

Stagger stance—The position an individual defensive player takes while guarding. In this stance, the player stands with his feet apart, one foot slightly ahead of the other. The hands are held at shoulder level ready to deflect passes.

Start the clock—After a timeout, the clock is started and play is resumed when the ball is tossed from a player who is out of bounds to a player on the court. The clock starts when the player on the court touches the ball.

Statistics—A written record of shots, rebounds, assists, errors, etc., that is used by coaches and sportswriters to evaluate teams. Professional and college statistics are published weekly in newspapers and magazines during the basketball season.

Stopping on a dime—Description given when a running player stops suddenly without falling forward.

Strong side—Description given to the side of the playing court where the ball is being handled.

Submarining—A defensive player runs under an offensive player who has jumped high into the air, causing the offensive player to fall. This is a dangerous play. The penalty is the awarding of two free shots to the offensive player. (See illustration)

Substitutes—Extra members of a team who sit on the players' bench with the coach. These players enter the game when their teammates on the floor need a rest or have fouled too many times and are disqualified from the game.

Superstars—The greatest high school, college, and professional players.

Sweep the boards—To jump higher than all players to grab a rebound.

Sweeping a series—When one team defeats another by winning all games in a series.

Switch—When two defensive players exchange opponents during a game.

T

Tap—Hitting the ball lightly so a teammate can easily catch it. This move is used during a tap play.

Tap Play—A play used during a jump ball situation. The jumping player signals to one of his teammates that he will tap the ball in his direction.

Team fouls—The total number of personal fouls committed by the players of a team.

Teamwork—Players of a team working together to score baskets and to stop the other team from scoring.

Technical foul—A technical foul is called by an official on the court when: 1) a player or team delays the game intentionally; 2) a team takes too many timeouts; 3) a player disobeys the game officials, or 4) a coach enters the playing court without the permission of the officials.

Telegraphing—When an offensive player makes it obvious to others where he is going to pass the ball.

Thirty-second rule—A rule which gives the offensive team only thirty seconds in which to attempt a shot at the basket. This rule is used only in women's basketball at the college level and in international competition.

Three-on-two—Three offensive players attacking the basket against only two defenders. This is usually the final play of a fast break.

Three point play—An offensive player makes a successful try for a basket and is fouled at the same time. The player then sinks a free throw for a total of three points.

Three second rule—Makes it illegal to remain in the free throw lane three seconds or more.

Three-two—A zone defense which uses three front players and two players near the basket. (See illustration)

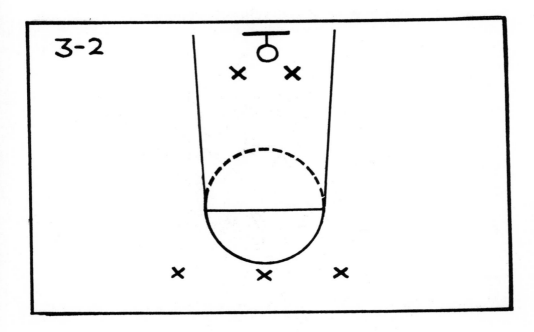

Timekeeper—The official who is in charge of starting and stopping the game clock. In leagues where shot clocks are used, additional officials are needed to operate them.

Timeout—A period of time in which the game clock is stopped for reason of injury, assessing fouls, or shooting free throws. A team may also call a timeout to rest its players or to talk about strategy.

Timing—The precise movement of players that makes an offensive play work perfectly.

Tip-in—An offensive rebound which is tapped back into the basket rather than grabbed and tossed to another player. A tip-in is considered a shot and is practiced by players.

Trailer—The fourth player downcourt on a fast break who usually trails the middle man. The trailer arrives at the basket to help the first group of players and to rebound if a shot is missed.

Trainer—The member of a team who takes care of the minor medical problems of the players. Most trainers are specialists who understand the treatment of athletic injuries.

Training Rules—Rules of discipline players must follow to keep in top physical condition. They are given to a team by its coach or captain.

Trap—When two defensive players double-team an offensive player who has the ball. They harass the player and try to cause him to make a bad pass or shot.

Traveling—When an offensive player illegally advances the ball by running or walking with it. The referee then blows his whistle, stops and gives the ball to the other team.

Triple screen—Similar to a double screen except that three players protect the shooter instead of two.

Try for a field goal—A shot at the basket from either far out or close to the basket.

Tryouts—Practice sessions held by coaches to select the best players for a team.

Turnovers—Errors that cause the offensive team to lose possession of the ball. The ball is then "turned over" to the opponents.

Twenty-four second rule—A rule which gives the offensive team twenty-four seconds in which to attempt a shot at the basket. This rule is used only by the NBA professional league.

Two-hand set shot—When a player stops, takes aim, and "gets set" before shooting the ball with two hands. This is an old-fashioned shot seldom used in modern basketball.

Two-one-two—A zone defense with two players up front, one in the free throw lane, and two under the basket. (See illustration)

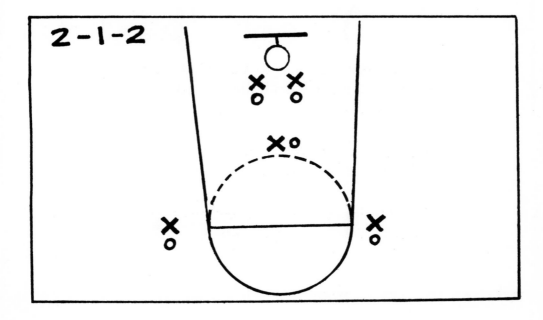

Two-two-one—A zone of defense with two players up front near the free throw circle, two players in the free throw lane, and one player under the basket. The player under the basket is usually the tallest. (See illustration)

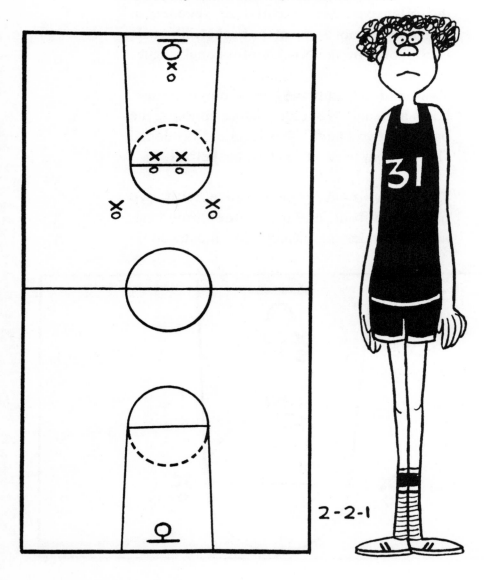

2-2-1

U

Umpire—One of two officials with a whistle who is on the court watching for fouls.

Underhand free throw—A type of free throw made with two hands. The player flips the ball up to the basket in an underhand motion while bending his knees. This shot, popular in the early years of basketball, is also called the "ape shot." (See illustration)

Underhand pass—Similar to the scoop and shovel pass, this pass can be made with one or two hands. It is used to give the ball to a cutting offensive player.

Unsportsmanlike conduct—Occurs when a player or a coach disrespectfully addresses an official, bumps an official while arguing with him, fights with an opponent, or uses profanity. A technical foul is charged against the offending player or coach.

Upcourt—The half of the playing court where the action is taking place.

V

Varsity—A team composed of the best players in a school. This team represents the school in games against other varsities.

V-cut—An offensive move used to escape a defensive player in order to receive a pass. The offensive player making this move runs a few steps towards the basket, then suddenly changes direction and heads towards a teammate with the ball. The path the player takes is v-shaped. (See illustration)

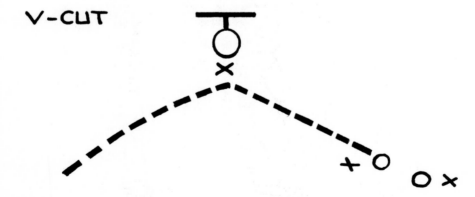

V-CUT

Violations—Infractions of the rules that result in loss of the ball rather than in free throws. Traveling, three seconds in the lane, and carrying the ball are common violations.

'HELD BALL'

Warm-up drills—Pre-game exercises performed by players in order to loosen their muscles for the game. Layups, light calisthenics, and shooting are some common warm-up drills.

Weak side—Description given to the side of the playing court where the ball is *not* being handled.

Weave—Three to five players controlling the ball. The players pass and move in a back and forth pattern near the sideline or close to the center of the court.

Weeding out—Eliminating players from a team who are either not needed or who do not play as well as the others.

Wheelchair basketball—A form of basketball played by people confined to wheelchairs because they have lost the use of their legs. These players wheel around the playing court, shoot, pass, and play defense. Tournaments for wheelchair teams are held at the end of each season.

Wing man—Another term for a forward. Also used to describe the outside players in one-three-one offense or defense. (See diagram, One-three-one)

X

X's and O's—The symbols used by coaches when drawing plays on a blackboard. The X's usually represent the defensive players and the O's the offensive players.

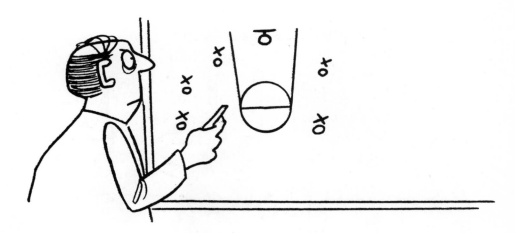

Z

Zone defense—A type of defense in which each defensive player guards a certain area of the court rather than an individual offensive player.

Zone offense—An offensive system used to attack a zone defense. Most teams have two or three different zone offenses to combat the many types of zone defenses.

Zone press—A type of zone defense. The players try to double team the offensive man with the ball and force him to make a bad pass. The remaining defensive players guard certain areas of the court and wait to deflect or intercept the ball.

WHO ARE the greatest basketball players of all time? There have been many since that cold, blustery day in 1891 when Dr. Naismith invented the game. Most of them (along with great basketball coaches) have been honored by being named to the Naismith Memorial Basketball Hall of Fame in Springfield, Massachusetts. Photos, life histories, statistics, plaques and other memorabilia of all these outstanding sports personalities are on display there. The beautiful Hall of Fame building is located near the original site where Dr. Naismith's gym class played the first basketball game.

One of basketball's greatest players was Bill Russell, the big center for the Champion Boston Celtics of the NBA professional league. During Russell's thirteen years as a professional player, his Celtics won the Nation Basketball Association's championship a record eleven times. The 6 foot 10 inch center was such a great leader that he was named the player-coach of the Celtics for the last three years of his professional career.

Winning championships was nothing new to Bill Russell. As the University of San Francisco's basketball star, he helped his team win an incredible 60 games in a row to capture the national college basketball championship. In 1956, the USA basketball team—led by Russell—won the Olympic gold medal at the Melbourne, Australia games.

Bill Russell is credited with changing the way in which centers are supposed to play basketball. For years, coaches told their centers to run downcourt, get position under the basket, and wait for high passes or for rebounds. On defense, centers used to play their position by just standing under the basket and clogging up the driving lanes to the hoop. But Russell added a new dimension to center play, the blocked shot.

Russell was a master at timing his leaps perfectly to reject attempted shots by frustrated opponents. Ever since Russell introduced the blocked shot as a prime defensive weapon, coaches have looked for centers with shot blocking ability.

As a further testimony to his greatness, Bill Russell was the only player unanimously selected by the sportswriters who chose the National Basketball Association's Silver Anniversary Team in 1971. This is an honorary team composed of the NBA's greatest stars.

Other great players from the past include Bob Cousy, George Mikan, Bob Pettit, Jerry West, Oscar Robertson, and Wilt Chamberlain. All of these "greats" have had an impact on the game of basketball.

Bob Cousy was one of professional basketball's first superstars. Standing only 6 feet tall, Cousy was called "Mr. Basketball" and "The Court Magician" because of his great passing and ball handling ability. It was Bob Cousy who first popularized the now common behind-the-back pass.

Cousy played with the Champion Boston Celtics as a teammate of Bill Russell. While captain of the Celtics, Cousy showed that there was a place in professional basketball for little men.

George Mikan, who played for the Champion Minneapolis Lakers in the early years of the NBA, was the first great tall man in professional basketball. At 6 feet 11 inches, Mikan was able to use his height and weight to good advantage under the basket. He popularized the sweeping hook shot.

Bob Pettit was a great forward for the St. Louis Hawks of the NBA. A deadly jump shooter and tough rebounder, Pettit was basketball's first superstar forward. Pettit was also voted to the National Basketball Association's Silver Anniversary Team.

Jerry West of the Los Angeles Lakers earned the nickname "Mr. Clutch" because of his great hustle and play during the final moments of close games. Before retiring in 1974, West was considered to be one of basketball's greatest guards. The 6 foot 4 inch sharpshooter's playing style has been copied, but never equalled, by many young professionals.

Oscar Robertson played for the Cincinnati Royals and the Milwaukee Bucks of the NBA. His nickname, "The Big O," shows the impact he had on basketball. While standing only 6 feet 5 inches, Robertson has been called the perfect all-around player. He could shoot, pass, rebound, dribble, and run on a par with the best players the game has known.

Another great player of the past is Wilt Chamberlain. Wilt "the Stilt" was the first giant center in basketball with giant ability to match. Combining tremendous strength with his 7 feet 2 inches, Chamberlain dominated the center position in the NBA.

Also called the "Big Dipper," Chamberlain filled arenas with eager fans who wanted to see the big center dunk the ball into the basket. Never before had a center controlled the offensive part of the game so totally. Wilt's greatest scoring achievement came in 1962 when he scored an unbelievable 100 points in a single NBA game. It is doubtful whether this record will ever be broken.

There are many young superstars today who are destined to be called "greats." The biggest and most notable of these players is Kareem Abdul Jabbar of the Los Angeles Lakers of the NBA. Standing 7 feet 3 inches tall, Jabbar has already been called the best player in the history of basketball. A rival coach recently said: "If you had to mold a player and say 'this is the perfect center,' it would be Kareem."

Bill Russell, now considered to be the best center who ever played, has said of Jabbar: "If he continues to improve, he will be the best ever." What makes Jabbar so great is his all around basketball ability. He can block shots like Russell, score points with regularity like Wilt "the Stilt", and, incredibly, can pass and dribble like a guard if necessary.

Jabbar was a basketball standout from the moment he played his first high school game in New York City. As a collegian, Jabbar led his UCLA team to three national college championships. As a pro, he has played so brilliantly and consistently that he is considered to be the best center in modern basketball.

Another great young center is Boston's Dave Cowens. At 6 feet 9 inches, Cowens proves a great center doesn't have to be over 7 feet to be successful. Cowens' hustling play both on offense and defense has won him acclaim from many coaches who once thought he was too small to be a good professional center.

Like another Boston center before him, Bill Russell, Cowens has changed the thinking of today's coaches. Because of Dave's ability to move quickly around bigger centers and to lead the fast break, small centers are now popular in professional basketball.

John Havlicek is on everybody's list of "great" players. Havlicek, a teammate of Cowens on the Celtics, has amazed basketball fans for years because of his great stamina. John has been called a machine because he seems to be able to run all during the game without tiring. Havlicek's inspired leadership of the Celtics has helped make Boston a powerful champion once again.

At 6 feet 5 inches, Havlicek can play either guard or forward. In fact, it was John's great play at either position that sent rival coaches searching for 6 foot 5 inch "swingmen," players who could perform well as a guard or a forward. Havlicek is also Boston's "Mr. Clutch." Like Jerry West of the Lakers, he is usually chosen by the Celtics to score the necessary points in crucial games.

Walt Frazier of the NBA New York Knicks is generally considered to be the best guard of the 1970's. A defensive standout, Walt is also the man the Knicks look to for scoring points in tough games. Frazier is the leader of the New York ball club.

Frazier is called "Mr. Cool" by his teammates. The 6 foot 4 inch guard never shows much emotion while playing. Maybe it's because the quick superstar is too busy guarding the other team's top scoring guard. Frazier has long been recognized as the best defensive guard in basketball.

Rick Barry of the NBA Golden State Warriors is one of basketball's best scorers. Whether close to the basket or far away, Barry has a knack for putting the ball into the hoop. He has won scoring championships in both the ABA and the NBA professional leagues, the only player to accomplish this feat.

One of basketball's best shooters is 6 foot 10 inch Bob McAdoo of the NBA New York Knicks. McAdoo uses his quickness to move around slower big men and has earned his reputation as the best shooting center in the NBA. McAdoo is one of the reasons the Knicks will always be a good team.

George McGinnis is one of basketball's youngest superstars. This muscular forward left Indiana University after his sophomore year to join the professional Indiana Pacers of the then ABA. He immediately became a star, rebounding and shooting like a seasoned veteran. He is so strong under the basket that few professional forwards like to challange "Big George" for rebounds. McGinnis now plays for the Philadelphia 76ers of the NBA.

Julius Erving of the Philadelphia team is one of the best players in the professional league. "Dr. J," as Erving is known, can do everything on the court and must be considered a basketball "great." A terrific shooter, "Dr. J" can also dribble, pass, and leap for rebounds.

Basketball is, of course, a team game. The greatest players cannot perform alone. They need teammates to pass the ball to them and to help on defense. In basketball, great *teams* win championships, not great players by themselves.

The greatest team of all time was the Boston Celtics team that played during the 1950's and 1960's. Led by Bob Cousy and Bill Russell, this superb unit dominated professional basketball. With great shooters like Sam Jones, Tom Heinsohn, and Bill Sharman, the Celtics had more scoring power than their NBA rivals. The coach of this great team was Arnold "Red" Auerbach, considered by many people to be the smartest professional coach in history.

Before the Celtics began their long domination of the NBA, the Minneapolis Lakers of 1948-53 were the undisputed champions of the league. Led by the first big basketball superstar, George Mikan, the Lakers were professional basketball's first powerhouse team. Jim Pollard, a tough forward, and little Slater Martin, a quick 5 foot 10 inch guard, helped Minneapolis clobber opponents.

College basketball has had its great teams, too. UCLA (the University of California at Los Angeles) dominated college championship tournaments during the 1960's and early 1970's. Kareem Abdul Jabbar, Sidney Wicks, Gail Goodrich, and Bill Walton are a few of the many great college players who played at UCLA. Ohio State, Notre Dame, and the University of Kentucky are other universities that always have powerful basketball teams. From these great college teams come the superstars of the future, the professional players who will someday be called "great."

Author STEVE CLARK, a native of Boston, Massachusetts, holds a degree in physical education from Butler University. His avid enthusiasm for basketball led him into coaching the sport in the United States, Mexico and England. He was the National Team Coach for the Dominican Republic, and El Salvador; and he has just returned from coaching Saudi Arabia's National Team.

Mr. Clark has written numerous articles on basketball and other topics for national and regional magazines. He currently lives in Massachusetts with his wife and two children, pursuing his careers of writing and coaching.

FRANK BAGINSKI uses his artistic talents in two fields. As an artist, his cartoons have appeared in major magazines and his comic strip, "Plain Jane", and his panel, "Little Emily", have been syndicated in newspapers throughout the country. He is a graduate of the School of Visual Arts in New York City. As an actor, Mr. Baginski works under the name Frank Aldrich and has recently completed parts in two movies. Mr. Baginski resides in New York City.

Manuel Moreno Guzmán